Preface

The Piano Workbooks

Teaching music can be a challenging task. To nurture a well-rounded musician, instructors must instill a sense of discipline without damping enthusiasm, and at the same time balance the study of repertoire with the study of technique. There is much to include in each weekly lesson and it is easy to sometimes focus on one area to the detriment of another, causing gaps in an otherwise solid education. *The Piano Workbook* has been developed in response to this need to "bring it all together".

Each level of the series, Preparatory to Level 10, includes a variety of teaching tools. Along with the assignment pages, there are checklists, charts, exercises and drills to make the job of organizing and guiding a student's musical journey easier. In addition, the Workbooks include the RCM 2015 Syllabus* technical and musicianship requirements as well as practicing grids for exam preparation. No other resource brings together as much to help students . . .

learn the notes, practice the piece and perform the music!

For other publications in the *Piano Workbook Series* see the back cover or visit www.pianoworkbook.com for more information and instructional videos.

---

* © 2015 The Frederick Harris Music Co., Limited, Toronto, Ontario, Canada. All rights reserved. Used with permission.

About the Author

Barbara M. Siemens is a piano instructor, author, clinician, and RCM Senior Examiner with over twenty five years of teaching experience. She holds a graduate degree in Historical Musicology, an ARCT Performer's Diploma and an ARCT Pedagogy Diploma for which she received the top standing in Canada. Ms. Siemens maintains a private studio in Vancouver where she works with students of all ages and abilities.

www.pianoworkbook.com

#180 - 6362 Fraser Street, Vancouver B.C., Canada, V5W 0A1

Table of Contents

PRACTICING STRATEGIES

GENERAL MUSICIANSHIP

TECHNIQUE

ASSIGNMENT RECORD

Practicing Strategies

Attach a customized

Studio Policy Statement

to this page.

Term I Goals

Dates for Term I _____

Practicing Plan:

Practicing Days _____

Length of Practice Sessions _____

Time of Day _____

Order of Practice Items _____

_____

Exam Preparation:

Date of Exam _____

Technique _____

Repertoire _____

_____

Studies _____

Sight Preparation _____

Ear Preparation _____

Theory Requirements _____

Public Performance: Date of Event _____

Repertoire _____

_____

Other Goals: Duets, Composition, etc. _____

_____

Student's Signature: _____

Term I Review: _____

_____

© 2015 Barbara M. Siemens PW-5x

Term II Goals

Dates for Term II _____

Practicing Plan: Practicing Days _____

Length of Practice Sessions _____

Time of Day _____

Order of Practice Items _____

_____

Exam Preparation: Date of Exam _____

Technique _____

Repertoire _____

_____

Studies _____

Sight Preparation _____

Ear Preparation _____

Theory Requirements _____

Public Performance: Date of Event _____

Repertoire _____

_____

Other Goals: Duets, Composition, etc. _____

_____

Student's Signature: _____

Term II Review: _____

_____

Term III Goals

Dates for Term III _____

Practicing Plan: Practicing Days _____

Length of Practice Sessions _____

Time of Day _____

Order of Practice Items _____

_____

Exam Preparation: Date of Exam _____

Technique _____

Repertoire _____

_____

Studies _____

Sight Preparation _____

Ear Preparation _____

Theory Requirements _____

Public Performance: Date of Event _____

Repertoire _____

_____

Other Goals: Duets, Composition, etc. _____

_____

Student's Signature: _____

Term III Review: _____

_____

© 2015 Barbara M. Siemens PW-5x

Virtuoso List

Title	Composer	Key	Date	Reminders

Bronze Level

	Title	Composer	Key	Date	Reminders
1.					
2.					
3.					
4.					
5.					
6.					

Silver Level

	Title	Composer	Key	Date	Reminders
7.					
8.					
9.					
10.					
11.					
12.					

Gold Level

	Title	Composer	Key	Date	Reminders
13.					
14.					
15.					
16.					
17.					
18.					

FIRST THINGS FIRST

Title
- understand the meaning

Composer
- note the name, dates, nationality

Musical Era
- find the composer's musical era

STUDY THE SCORE

Key Signature
- note the sharps or flats and name the key
- play through the tonic scale and the tonic triad in inversions

Time Signature
- understand the basic beat and the break-down of the basic beat

Form
- look for the structure

Counting
- write in the counting

Difficult Rhythms
- counting out loud, clap difficult sections 3x, 5x, or until secure

Sections
- divide the piece into 2 bar, 4 bar, 8 bar sections

Terms
- define all the musical terms on the score
- use the *Music Glossary* if necessary

Unusual Features
- look for accidentals, ledger lines, changes in clefs, hand crossings, etc.

LEARN THE NOTES

In Sections
- work in sections
- start hands separate, repeat 3x, 5x, or until secure
- play slowly and accurately
- play to the first beat of the next section or bar

Follow the Score
- check for:
  a) notes
  b) fingering
  c) rhythm
  d) articulation
  e) basic dynamic colour

Count Out Loud
- count out loud to establish a firm pulse and accurate rhythm

Find the Patterns
- look for:
  a) scales
  b) triads
  c) repetitions
  d) other groupings

Difficult Spots
- find challenging passages, circle or mark them with a coloured dot
- practice these sections first and repeat them more often

© 2015 Barbara M. Siemens PW-5x

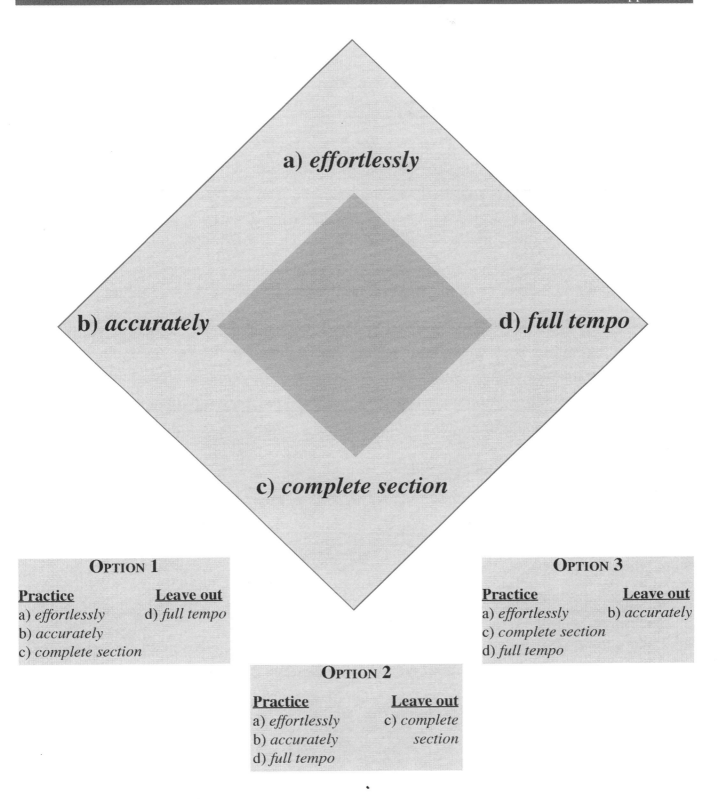

a) *effortlessly*

b) *accurately*

d) *full tempo*

c) *complete section*

OPTION 1

Practice	Leave out
a) *effortlessly*	d) *full tempo*
b) *accurately*	
c) *complete section*	

OPTION 2

Practice	Leave out
a) *effortlessly*	c) *complete*
b) *accurately*	*section*
d) *full tempo*	

OPTION 3

Practice	Leave out
a) *effortlessly*	b) *accurately*
c) *complete section*	
d) *full tempo*	

* Quoted with permission from *Effortless Mastery: Liberating the Musician Within* by Kenny Werner, published by Jamey Aebersold Jazz Inc, New Albany In., USA, 1996.

FIRST THINGS FIRST

Fingering	• check for accuracy
Key Signature	• state the sharps and flats
Metronome	• use it to maintain the pulse
Count Out Loud	• count out loud with or without the metronome

THE BASICS

Diagnosis	• find the problem, find an exercise, practice the passage, review and repeat
Eyes Closed	• play with eyes closed
Reverse Direction	• play descending first, then ascending
Two-in-a-Row	• play twice in a row, at top speed, without pauses
Articulation	• play staccato
Fallboard Practice	• play on the fallboard or a table top
H.S.	• secure the hands separately

TECHNICAL ISSUES

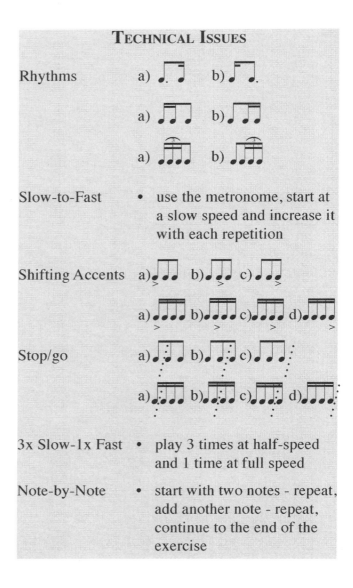

Rhythms	
Slow-to-Fast	• use the metronome, start at a slow speed and increase it with each repetition
Shifting Accents	
Stop/go	
3x Slow-1x Fast	• play 3 times at half-speed and 1 time at full speed
Note-by-Note	• start with two notes - repeat, add another note - repeat, continue to the end of the exercise

SPECIFIC SUGGESTIONS

Scales	• block the black keys
	• block the 6th and 7th notes
	• stop on the tonic notes and check the fingering
	• repeat the *turn around*
Arpeggios	• name notes while playing
Triads	• broken/solid practice
	• 3*2*1

© 2015 Barbara M. Siemens PW-5x

FIRST THINGS FIRST

Concentrate
- think, then play

Ask Questions
- Was that secure enough? Is the articulation exact? Were the phrases musical? etc.

Diagnosis
- find the problem, find an exercise, practice the passage, review and repeat

TECHNICAL ISSUES

Technique
- use the practicing tools listed on page 14

Staccato Work
- play legato passages with staccato articulation

Blocking
- block broken triads, and Alberti patterns

Fallboard Practice
- practice on the fallboard

THE BASICS

Accuracy
- follow the score markings

Hands Separate
- practice hands separate, as well as hands together

Count Out Loud
- say the rhythm out loud for a secure pulse

Metronome
- use it to maintain the pulse

Control
- maintain a controlled tempo

Sections
- practice in sections and bracket them with post-its on the score

Repetitions
- accurately repeat passages 3x, 5x or until the desired effect is achieved

Patterns
- look for scales, triads, arpeggios, sequences, repeated figures, etc.

Dynamics
- follow the dynamics, use *Descriptive Words* to create memorable images

Werner Diamond
- refer to page 13

RHYTHMIC ISSUES

Clapping
- clap the rhythm while counting out loud

Tapping
- tap the basic beat with one hand and the rhythm in the other hand, reverse the parts and repeat

Word Play
- use imaginative sentences or words to remember problematic rhythms

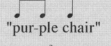

"pur-ple chair"

"move a-long fast"

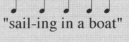

"sail-ing in a boat"

"wait and then go"

"sas-ka-toon pie"

BASIC STRATEGIES

Divide the Piece
- divide the score into sections
- number each one to create a starting point

Hands Separate
- be able to play either hand alone by memory

Security
- work slowly and carefully
- do memory work at the beginning of a practice session, when the mind is fresh

Review
- review new memory work later in the same practice session
- review with patient, it takes several sessions for short-term memory work to shift into long-term memory

ANALYTICAL MEMORY

Key Signature
- know the key signature, tonic scale and tonic triad

Time Signature
- understand the time signature and all rhythmic patterns

Modulations
- look for accidentals that indicate modulations
- know the relevant scales and triads

Harmony
- use the harmony to relate the music to the tonic/dominant notes and triads

Form
- know the structure and find the important features, i.e. themes, subjects, etc.

Patterns
- look for sequences, scales, arpeggios, triads, etc.

MUSCLE MEMORY

Small Muscles
- repeat passages many times over a number of days, weeks, and months to train the finger memory
- counter each inaccurate repetition with 5 or more accurate repetitions

Large Muscles
- repeat large leaps many times with eyes open and then closed to train the arm muscle memory

AT HOME

Memory Work
- use the ideas on page 16

Starting Points
- be able to begin at all starting points, especially the weaker sections
- practice moving from one starting point to the next, without pausing

Hands Separate
- by able to play the entire piece hands separate by memory

Count Out Loud
- count out loud while playing by memory to test the rhythmic and metric clarity

Without Sight
- play with eyes closed, use a tempo slower than the performance speed

Without Sound
- play by memory on the fallboard
- try hands separate and hands together, review any passage than can not be clearly remembered

Self-Recording
- record your performance, listen for both strong and weak areas

Performing
- try all of the following:
  a) one shot performances
  b) cold starts
  c) practice recitals

FOR THE EVENT

That Day
- avoid sugar or pop
- warm-up thoroughly without doing anything too strenuous

At the Event
- arrive early to avoid panic
- wear extra clothing or gloves to keep warm before playing
- sit quietly and avoid unnecessary conversation
- use a deep breathing exercise to bring oxygen to the brain and extremities:
  a) breathe in deeply through the nose and pause for 3 seconds,
  b) breathe out slowly through the mouth and pause for 3 seconds,
  c) repeat 5 to 10 times.

The Routine
- use the following ideas to create a performance routine:
  a) walk slowly to the piano
  b) bow
  c) adjust the chair
  d) think before playing
  e) breathe before playing
  f) perform the music
  g) pause before standing
  h) bow, walk slowly back

MAJOR KEY
Fast Tempo

bold	jolly
bright	joyful
brisk	laughing
bubbly	lively
bumpy	merrily
cheerful	playful
crisp	powerful
dancing	racing
delightful	rippling
energetic	shimmering
exciting	spirited
funny	sunny
galloping	
happy	
huge	
hurried	
jittery	
joking	

MAJOR KEY
Slow Tempo

angelic	loving
bell-like	magical
calm	peaceful
carefree	rolling
careful	singing
charming	sleepy
delicate	smooth
dreamy	sticky
drifting	sweetly
expressive	tender
floating	tired
friendly	whispering
gentle	
gliding	
graceful	
heavenly	
hopeful	
light	

MINOR KEY
Fast Tempo

angry	nervous
annoyed	pounding
anxious	prickly
desperate	raging
crazy	roaring
explosive	scary
fearful	scowling
forceful	spikey
frightening	stormy
furious	surprised
greedy	terrified
hasty	towering
horrified	
howling	
irritated	
jumpy	
mad	
nasty	

MINOR KEY
Slow Tempo

awkward	mysterious
bewildered	pathetic
complaining	pleading
creepy	pouting
dark	resigned
depressed	rocking
desolate	sad
foggy	scolding
ghostly	stomping
gloomy	tragic
grumpy	whimpering
heavy	whining
intense	
lost	
marching	
misty	
moping	
murky	

18

General Musicianship

BAROQUE C.1600 - 1750

Composers   J.S. Bach, C.P.E Bach, J.C. Bach, Couperin, Graupner, Handel, Pachelbel, Purcell, Rameau, Scarlatti, Telemann, Zipoli . . .

Style
- interesting left hand and right hand parts (contrapuntal texture)
- staccato in one hand versus legato in the other for contrast
- narrow dynamic range, *p* to *f*
- dynamics in blocks (terraced)
- few, if any performance directions

Forms
- A B form for dances: minuet, bourrée, gigue, polonaise, allemande, sarabande . . .
- prelude . . .

Instruments
- harpsichord
- clavichord
- organ

CLASSICAL C.1770 - 1820

Composers   Beethoven, Clementi, Czerny, Diabelli, Dussek, Haydn, Kuhlau, Mozart . . .

Style
- triads in one hand versus melody in the other (homophonic texture)
- sudden changes in rhythms for contrast
- more dynamic changes
- steady tempo
- some performance directions

Forms
- sonatina
- rondo
- theme with variations. . .

Instruments - forte-piano

ROMANTIC/POST ROMANTIC C.1820 - 1910

Composers   Chopin, Gedike, Gretchaninov, Gurlitt, Reinecke, Schubert, Schumann, Tchaikovsky . . .

Style
- projected melodies
- longer phrases
- some rhythmic flexibility
- wider dynamic range
- use of damper and *una corda* pedals
- descriptive titles
- more specific performance directions

Forms
- A B A ternary form
- through-composed
- character pieces

Instruments
- piano-forte or grand piano
- upright piano

20TH CENTURY/CONTEMPORARY

Composers   Bartók, Berlin, Gillock, Kabalevsky, Mier, Nakada, Niamath, Pinto, Shostakovich, Starer, Tan, Tansman . . .

Style
- clusters
- melodic clashes (dissonance)
- whole tone, modal, blues scales
- styles from previous eras
- nationalistic or folk styles
- novel use of the piano
- very precise performance directions

Forms
- any form from earlier eras

Instruments
- modern grand and upright pianos
- electric piano
- disklavier
- synthesizer

Theory References

TIME SIGNATURES

Simple Time

Compound Time

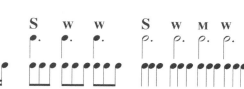

IRREGULAR GROUPINGS AND DOTS

Triplets and Duplets

Dots

COMMON FORMS

- Binary: *A B*

- Ternary: *A B A*

- Rondo: *A B A C A B A*

- Theme and Variations

- Sonata allegro form: see the "house" diagram

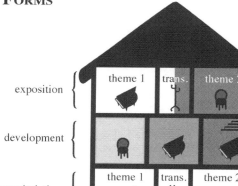

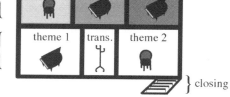

TRIADS AND CHORDS

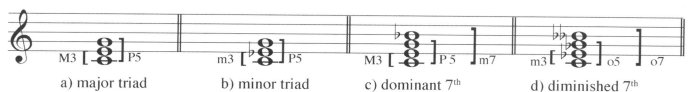

a) major triad   b) minor triad   c) dominant 7th   d) diminished 7th

---

© 2015 Barbara M. Siemens PW-5x

Theory References

MAJOR KEYS

C (0)

F (1)   G (1)

B♭ (2)   D (2)

E♭ (3)   Circle of Fifths   A (3)

A♭ (4)   E (4)

D♭ (5)   B (5)
C♯ (7)   C♭ (7)

G♭ (6)
F♯ (6)

Order of the *SHARPS* and *FLATS*

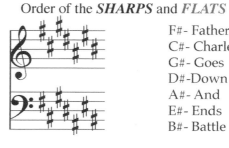

F#- Father
C#- Charles
G#- Goes
D#-Down
A#- And
E#- Ends
B#- Battle

B♭- Battle
E♭- Ends
A♭- And
D♭- Down
G♭- Goes
C♭- Charles'
F♭- Father

MINOR KEYS

MINOR KEY SIGNATURES

- Each minor key is related to a major key; the two related keys have the same key signature.

- To find the minor scale's tonic, start on the tonic of a major scale and count to its 6th degree (submediant).

MINOR SCALES

- Natural minor — no alterations

- Harmonic minor — raise the 7th note

- Melodic minor — raise the 6th and 7th notes up
  — lower the 6th and 7th notes down

CADENCES

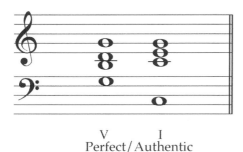

V   I
Perfect/Authentic

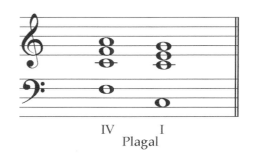

IV   I
Plagal

RHYTHM DRILLS

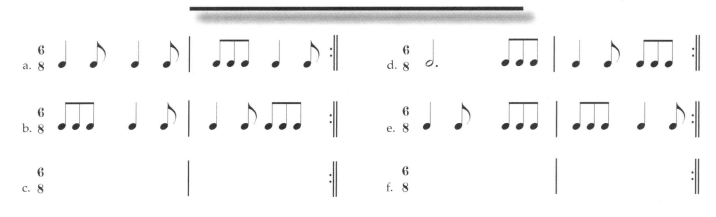

© 2015 Barbara M. Siemens PW-5x

Rhythm Exercises

RHYTHM EXAMPLES: CLAP ONE OR MIX AND MATCH TWO AT A TIME

STUDY THE SCORE

Key Signature	• list the sharps or flats, state the major or minor key
Accidentals	• look for accidentals, carry them through the bar
Time Signature	• determine the meter and the number of beats per bar
Rhythm	• clap and count the first phrase, find the difficult passages
Notes	• look at the notes for both hands, especially in the first and last bars
	• finger through the piece
	• search for scales, triads, sequences, patterns, or repetitions
	• check for intervals outside of the five finger position
	• note any ledger lines
Tempo	• check the tempo markings
Score Markings	• note the articulation, fingering and dynamics

PLAY THE PIECE

Count Out Loud	• count in to begin and continue through the piece
Read Ahead	• look a half or full bar ahead
Avoid Pauses	• do not pause to find notes or correct mistakes
Leave Notes Out	• leave notes out to maintain the pulse
Final Note	• hold the final note full value

OTHER STRATEGIES

Regular Practice	• sight read daily or every other day
Sight Exercises	• use the exercises on page 27
Rhythm Exercises	• use the exercises on pages 24-25
Eyes on the Score	• keep the eyes on the score by covering the hands with a light towel or an opaque plastic bag
Metronome	• maintain a secure pulse
Vertical Pacer	• have someone cover the notes already played in score with a vertical pacer (piece of paper, book, etc.)
Quick Studies	• learn a quick study over a week with accurate notes, fingering, rhythm, articulation and dynamics
Duets	• play duets with the teacher or another musician

6 NOTE PATTERNS

HARMONIC INTERVALS

CHROMATIC NOTES

Interval Exercises

major 2

do re   do re   do re mi   do re mi   do re   do

major 6

do la   do la so la do do   do la so la   do

minor 2

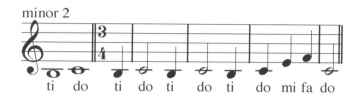

ti do   ti do   ti do   ti do   mi fa do

minor 6

la fa   la fa fa fa la la   la fa so   la

major 3

do mi   do mi   mi do   do mi mi   mi do do

major 7

do ti   do ti do   do ti do   ti   do

minor 3

la do   la do mi   la do mi   la do do   do la la

minor 7

so fa   so ti re   fa so fa   fa re ti   so

perfect 4

do fa   do fa   do fa so   do fa so fa   do do

perfect 8

do do   do do do   do do do   do do   do do   do do do

perfect 5

do so   do so   do so   do so so   so do do

Interval Exercises

RHYTHMS IN 2/4, 3/4, 4/4

a. b. c. d.

e. f.

RHYTHMS IN 6/8

a. b. c.

BASICS

- Keys — C, G, F, D
- Intervals — 2nd, 3rd, 5th, 8^{ve}

PARAMETERS

- Range — I to I; start on I, III, or V
- Span — 6 notes

HARMONIC PLAYBACKS

- Keys   — G, F, D
- Intervals   — M2, M3, P4
              P5, M6, P8
- Parameters — 3 intervals,
              within I to I

Example

MELODIC PLAYBACKS

- Keys   — C, G, F, G
- Range   — I to I
- Parameters — 7 notes,

Example

TRIAD PLAYBACKS

- Keys   — C, G, F, D
- Triads   — major, minor,
              diminished
- Parameters — 4 triads

Example

© 2015 Barbara M. Siemens PW-5x

ACCOMPANIMENT PATTERNS

SCALES

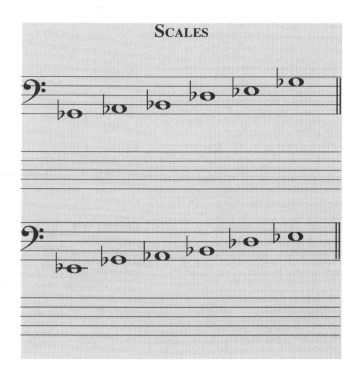

© 2015 Barbara M. Siemens PW-5x

Technique

Other Keys

Previous Level *

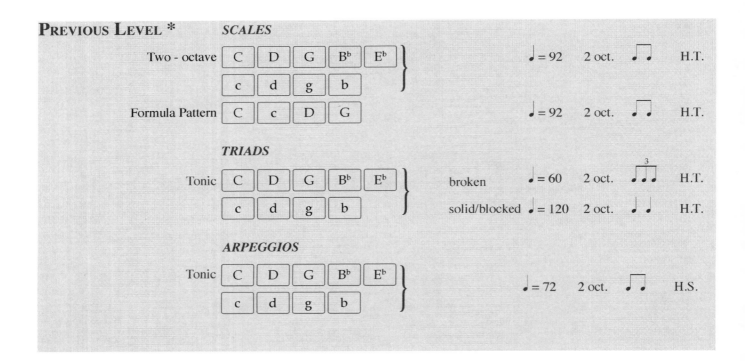

SCALES

Two - octave	C	D	G	B♭	E♭	}	♩ = 92	2 oct.	♪♪	H.T.
	c	d	g	b						
Formula Pattern	C	c	D	G			♩ = 92	2 oct.	♪♪	H.T.

TRIADS

Tonic	C	D	G	B♭	E♭	}	broken	♩ = 60	2 oct.	♪♪♪ (3)	H.T.
	c	d	g	b			solid/blocked	♩ = 120	2 oct.	♩ ♩	H.T.

ARPEGGIOS

Tonic	C	D	G	B♭	E♭	}	♩ = 72	2 oct.	♪♪	H.S.
	c	d	g	b						

Next Level *

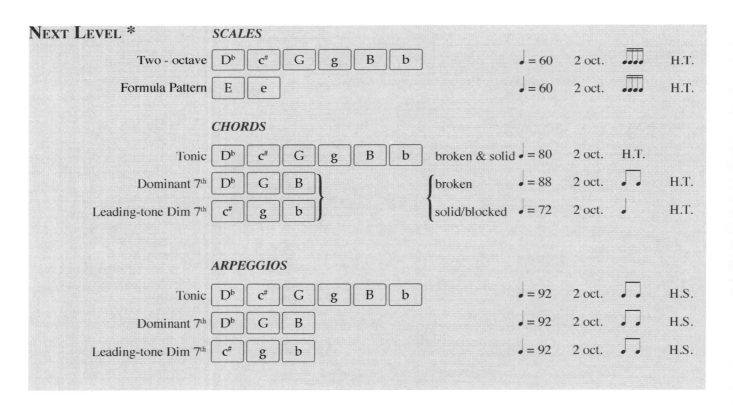

SCALES

Two - octave	D♭	c♯	G	g	B	b	♩ = 60	2 oct.	♪♪♪♪	H.T.
Formula Pattern	E	e					♩ = 60	2 oct.	♪♪♪♪	H.T.

CHORDS

Tonic	D♭	c♯	G	g	B	b	broken & solid	♩ = 80	2 oct.		H.T.
Dominant 7th	D♭	G	B		}	broken	♩ = 88	2 oct.	♪♪	H.T.
Leading-tone Dim 7th	c♯	g	b			solid/blocked	♩ = 72	2 oct.	♩	H.T.

ARPEGGIOS

Tonic	D♭	c♯	G	g	B	b	♩ = 92	2 oct.	♪♪	H.S.
Dominant 7th	D♭	G	B			♩ = 92	2 oct.	♪♪	H.S.
Leading-tone Dim 7th	c♯	g	b			♩ = 92	2 oct.	♪♪	H.S.

* Keys from other levels that are duplciated in the Level 5 requirements are not included. Refer to the syllabus for full details.

TECHNICAL TESTS

SCALES

Two - octave	A, E, F, A♭	♩ = 104	2 oct.		H.T.		
	a, e, f	♩ = 104	2 oct.		H.T. harmonic and melodic form		
Formula Pattern	A, a	♩ = 104	2 oct.		H.T. harmonic form		
Chromatic	A, F	♩ = 104	1 oct.		H.T.		

CHORDS

Tonic Triad (I V I)	A, E, F, A♭	♩ = 66	2 oct.		H.T. broken	
	a, e, f	♩ = 66	2 oct.		H.T. solid/blocked	
Dominant 7th	A, E, F, A♭	♩ = 72	1 oct.		H.S. broken	
		♩ = 60	1 oct.		H.S. solid/blocked	

ARPEGGIOS

Tonic	A, E, F, A♭	♩ = 80	2 oct.		H.S.	
	a, e, f	♩ = 80	2 oct.		H.S.	

MUSICIANSHIP

EAR TESTS

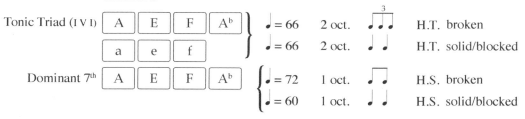

Intervals: M3 m3 P4 P5 M6 m6 P8   Identify intervals played in melodic/harmonic form.

Chords: M m triads   V⁷ 7th chord   Identify chords played in blocked form.

Chord Progression: I IV I   I V I   Identify chord progressions in a major key.

Playback: A a E e   Clap back the rhythm of a melody starting on I, III, V or I; then play it.

SIGHT READING

In a Level 2 passage, major or minor key with up to 2 sharps or flats; tap the rhythm and a steady beat; then play the passage.

REPERTOIRE

List A _____   Etude _____

List B _____   Etude _____

List C _____

*   © 2015 The Frederick Harris Music Co., Limited, Toronto, Ontario, Canada. All rights reserved. Used with permission.
    Refer to the 2015 Piano Syllabus for full details. Refer to the current RCM Theory Syllabus for written co-requistes.

DAY 1

Major Scales ☐☐

Minor Scales ☐☐

Formula Pattern ☐☐

Chromatic ☐☐

Triads ☐☐

Dominant 7ths ☐☐

Arpeggios ☐☐

DAY 2

Major Scales ☐☐

Minor Scales ☐☐

Formula Pattern ☐☐

Chromatic ☐☐

Triads ☐☐

Dominant 7ths ☐☐

Arpeggios ☐☐

DAY 3

Major Scales ☐☐

Minor Scales ☐☐

Formula Pattern ☐☐

Chromatic ☐☐

Triads ☐☐

Dominant 7ths ☐☐

Arpeggios ☐☐

DAY 4

Major Scales ☐☐

Minor Scales ☐☐

Formula Pattern ☐☐

Chromatic ☐☐

Triads ☐☐

Dominant 7ths ☐☐

Arpeggios ☐☐

DAY 5

Major Scales ☐☐

Minor Scales ☐☐

Formula Pattern ☐☐

Chromatic ☐☐

Triads ☐☐

Dominant 7ths ☐☐

Arpeggios ☐☐

DAY 6

Major Scales ☐☐

Minor Scales ☐☐

Formula Pattern ☐☐

Chromatic ☐☐

Triads ☐☐

Dominant 7ths ☐☐

Arpeggios ☐☐

© 2015 Barbara M. Siemens PW-5x

	Sept.	Oct.	Nov.	Dec.	Jan.	Feb.	Mar.	Apr.	May	June	July	Aug.

SCALES

Major												
Minor												
Forumla Pattern												
Chromatic												

CHORDS

Tonic - broken												
Tonic - solid												
Dominant 7th - broken												
Dominant 7th - solid												

APREGGIOS

Tonic												

SCALES - H.T.

	LEFT HAND		RIGHT HAND	
C, D, E, G, A c, d, e, g, a	• start on 5	cross 3 - 4 - 3	• start on 1	cross 3 - 4 - 3
B, b	• start on 4	cross 4 - 3 - 4	• start on 1	cross 3 - 4 - 3
F f	• start on 5	cross 3 - 4 - 3	• start on 1	cross 4 - 3 - 4
B♭, A♭ c#(h)	• start on 3	cross 4 - 3 - 4	• start on 2	cross 3 - 4 - 3
c# (m)	• start on 3	cross 4 - 3 - 4	• start on 2	cross 4 - 3 - 4 up cross 3 - 4 - 3 down
D♭, E♭	• start on 3	cross 4 - 3 - 4	• start on 2	cross 4 - 3 - 4

TRIADS - H.T.

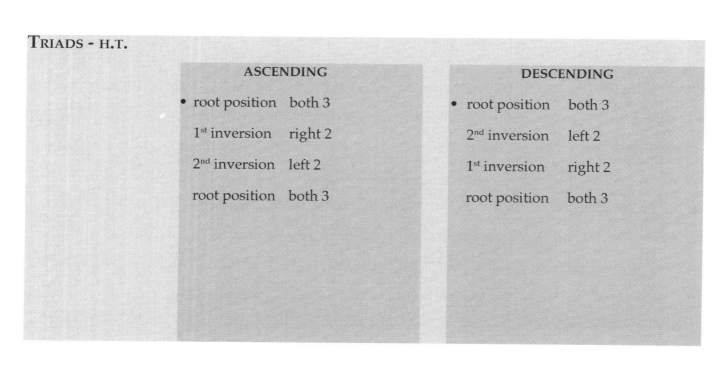

ASCENDING		DESCENDING	
• root position	both 3	• root position	both 3
1st inversion	right 2	2nd inversion	left 2
2nd inversion	left 2	1st inversion	right 2
root position	both 3	root position	both 3

40

© 2015 Barbara M. Siemens PW-5x

CHORDS - H.S.

DOMINANT 7ths	LEFT HAND		RIGHT HAND	
	• root position	5 - 4$^{(3)}$ - 2 - 1	• root position	1 - 2 - 4$^{(3)}$ - 5
	1st inversion	5 - 4 - 2 - 1	1st inversion	1 - 2 - 4 - 5
	2nd inversion	5 - 3 - 2 - 1	2nd inversion	1 - 2 - 3 - 5
	3rd position	5 - 4 - 2 - 1	3rd inversion	1 - 2 - 4 - 5
	root position	5 - 4$^{(3)}$ - 2 - 1	root position	1 - 2 - 4$^{(3)}$ - 5

ARPEGGIOS - H.S.

	LEFT HAND		RIGHT HAND	
C, D, E, F, G, A, B c, d, e, f, g, a, b	• start on 5	cross 4 - 2 - 1	• start on 1	cross 1 - 2 - 3
D^b, E^b, A^b c#, f#	• start on 2	cross 4 - 2 - 1	• start on 2	cross 1 - 2 - 4

© 2015 Barbara M. Siemens PW-5x

Assignment Record

Lesson 1 _____ _____	Lesson 24 _____ _____
Lesson 2 _____ _____	Lesson 25 _____ _____
Lesson 3 _____ _____	Lesson 26 _____ _____
Lesson 4 _____ _____	Lesson 27 _____ _____
Lesson 5 _____ _____	Lesson 28 _____ _____
Lesson 6 _____ _____	Lesson 29 _____ _____
Lesson 7 _____ _____	Lesson 30 _____ _____
Lesson 8 _____ _____	Lesson 31 _____ _____
Lesson 9 _____ _____	Lesson 32 _____ _____
Lesson 10 _____ _____	Lesson 33 _____ _____
Lesson 11 _____ _____	Lesson 34 _____ _____
Lesson 12 _____ _____	Lesson 35 _____ _____
Lesson 13 _____ _____	Lesson 36 _____ _____
Lesson 14 _____ _____	Lesson 37 _____ _____
Lesson 15 _____ _____	Lesson 38 _____ _____
Lesson 16 _____ _____	Lesson 39 _____ _____
Lesson 17 _____ _____	Lesson 40 _____ _____
Lesson 18 _____ _____	Lesson 41 _____ _____
Lesson 19 _____ _____	Lesson 42 _____ _____
Lesson 20 _____ _____	Lesson 43 _____ _____
Lesson 21 _____ _____	Lesson 44 _____ _____
Lesson 22 _____ _____	Lesson 45 _____ _____
Lesson 23 _____ _____	Lesson 46 _____ _____

Title/Composer	Date	H.S.	H.T.	Memory

Date

	M.M.	Reps.	Sun.	Mon.	Tues.	Wed.	Thurs.	Fri.	Sat.
Ear Training									
Sight Reading									
Technique									
Repertoire									

Theory _____

Next Lesson _____

Date

	M.M.	Reps.	Sun.	Mon.	Tues.	Wed.	Thurs.	Fri.	Sat.

Ear Training _____

Sight Reading _____

Technique _____

_____

_____

_____

Repertoire

_____

_____

_____

_____

_____

_____

_____

_____

_____

_____

_____

_____

_____

_____

_____

_____

Theory _____

Next Lesson _____

Date

	M.M.	Reps.	Sun.	Mon.	Tues.	Wed.	Thurs.	Fri.	Sat.
Ear Training _____									
Sight Reading _____									
Technique _____									
_____									
_____									
_____									

Repertoire

	M.M.	Reps.	Sun.	Mon.	Tues.	Wed.	Thurs.	Fri.	Sat.
_____									
_____									

_____

	M.M.	Reps.	Sun.	Mon.	Tues.	Wed.	Thurs.	Fri.	Sat.
_____									
_____									

_____

	M.M.	Reps.	Sun.	Mon.	Tues.	Wed.	Thurs.	Fri.	Sat.
_____									
_____									

_____

	M.M.	Reps.	Sun.	Mon.	Tues.	Wed.	Thurs.	Fri.	Sat.
_____									
_____									

_____

	M.M.	Reps.	Sun.	Mon.	Tues.	Wed.	Thurs.	Fri.	Sat.
_____									
_____									

_____

Theory _____

Next Lesson _____

Date

	M.M.	Reps.	Sun.	Mon.	Tues.	Wed.	Thurs.	Fri.	Sat.
Ear Training _____									
Sight Reading _____									
Technique _____									
_____									
_____									
_____									

Repertoire

Theory _____

Next Lesson _____

© 2015 Barbara M. Siemens PW-5x

Date

	M.M.	Reps.	Sun.	Mon.	Tues.	Wed.	Thurs.	Fri.	Sat.

Ear Training _____

Sight Reading _____

Technique _____

_____

_____

_____

Repertoire

_____

_____

_____

_____

_____

_____

_____

_____

_____

_____

_____

_____

_____

_____

_____

Theory _____

Next Lesson _____

Date

	M.M.	Reps.	Sun.	Mon.	Tues.	Wed.	Thurs.	Fri.	Sat.
Ear Training									
Sight Reading									
Technique									

Repertoire

Theory _____

Next Lesson _____

	M.M.	Reps.	Sun.	Mon.	Tues.	Wed.	Thurs.	Fri.	Sat.
Ear Training									
Sight Reading									
Technique									
Repertoire									

Theory _____

Next Lesson _____

Date

	M.M.	Reps.	Sun.	Mon.	Tues.	Wed.	Thurs.	Fri.	Sat.
Ear Training									
Sight Reading									
Technique									

Repertoire

Theory

Next Lesson

Date

	M.M.	Reps.	Sun.	Mon.	Tues.	Wed.	Thurs.	Fri.	Sat.

Ear Training _____

Sight Reading _____

Technique _____

_____

_____

_____

Repertoire

_____

_____

_____

_____

_____

_____

_____

_____

_____

_____

_____

_____

_____

_____

_____

Theory _____

Next Lesson _____

Date

	M.M.	Reps.	Sun.	Mon.	Tues.	Wed.	Thurs.	Fri.	Sat.
Ear Training _____									
Sight Reading _____									
Technique _____									
_____									
_____									
_____									

Repertoire									
_____									
_____									

Theory _____

Next Lesson _____

Date

	M.M.	Reps.	Sun.	Mon.	Tues.	Wed.	Thurs.	Fri.	Sat.

Ear Training _____

Sight Reading _____

Technique _____

_____

_____

_____

Repertoire

_____

_____

_____

_____

_____

_____

_____

_____

_____

_____

_____

_____

_____

_____

_____

_____

_____

_____

Theory _____

Next Lesson _____

Date

	M.M.	Reps.	Sun.	Mon.	Tues.	Wed.	Thurs.	Fri.	Sat.

Ear Training _____

Sight Reading _____

Technique _____

_____

_____

_____

Repertoire

_____

_____

_____

_____

_____

_____

_____

_____

_____

_____

_____

_____

_____

Theory _____

Next Lesson _____

Date

	M.M.	Reps.	Sun.	Mon.	Tues.	Wed.	Thurs.	Fri.	Sat.

Ear Training _____

Sight Reading _____

Technique _____

_____

_____

_____

Repertoire

_____

_____

_____

_____

_____

_____

_____

_____

_____

_____

_____

_____

_____

_____

_____

_____

_____

_____

Theory _____

Next Lesson _____

Date

	M.M.	Reps.	Sun.	Mon.	Tues.	Wed.	Thurs.	Fri.	Sat.
Ear Training _____									
Sight Reading _____									
Technique _____									
_____									
_____									
_____									
Repertoire _____									
_____									
_____									
_____									
_____									
_____									
_____									
_____									
_____									
_____									
_____									

Theory _____

Next Lesson _____

© 2015 Barbara M. Siemens PW-5x

Date

	M.M.	Reps.	Sun.	Mon.	Tues.	Wed.	Thurs.	Fri.	Sat.

Ear Training _____

Sight Reading _____

Technique _____

_____

_____

_____

Repertoire

_____

_____

_____

_____

_____

_____

_____

_____

_____

_____

_____

_____

_____

_____

Theory _____

Next Lesson _____

Date

	M.M.	Reps.	Sun.	Mon.	Tues.	Wed.	Thurs.	Fri.	Sat.

Ear Training _____

Sight Reading _____

Technique _____

_____

_____

_____

Repertoire

_____

_____

_____

_____

_____

_____

_____

_____

_____

_____

_____

_____

_____

_____

_____

_____

Theory _____

Next Lesson _____

© 2015 Barbara M. Siemens PW-5x

Date

	M.M.	Reps.	Sun.	Mon.	Tues.	Wed.	Thurs.	Fri.	Sat.
Ear Training									
Sight Reading									
Technique									

Repertoire

	M.M.	Reps.	Sun.	Mon.	Tues.	Wed.	Thurs.	Fri.	Sat.

Theory _____

Next Lesson _____

Date

	M.M.	Reps.	Sun.	Mon.	Tues.	Wed.	Thurs.	Fri.	Sat.

Ear Training _____

Sight Reading _____

Technique _____

_____

_____

_____

Repertoire

_____

_____

_____

_____

_____

_____

_____

_____

_____

_____

_____

_____

_____

_____

_____

_____

Theory _____

Next Lesson _____

Date

	M.M.	Reps.	Sun.	Mon.	Tues.	Wed.	Thurs.	Fri.	Sat.

Ear Training _____

Sight Reading _____

Technique _____

_____

_____

_____

Repertoire

_____

_____

_____

_____

_____

_____

_____

_____

_____

_____

_____

_____

_____

_____

_____

_____

Theory _____

Next Lesson _____

Date

	M.M.	Reps.	Sun.	Mon.	Tues.	Wed.	Thurs.	Fri.	Sat.
Ear Training									
Sight Reading									
Technique									

Repertoire

Theory _____

Next Lesson _____

Date

	M.M.	Reps.	Sun.	Mon.	Tues.	Wed.	Thurs.	Fri.	Sat.

Ear Training _____

Sight Reading _____

Technique _____

_____

_____

_____

Repertoire

_____

_____

_____

_____

_____

_____

_____

_____

_____

_____

_____

_____

_____

_____

_____

Theory _____

Next Lesson _____

Date

	M.M.	Reps.	Sun.	Mon.	Tues.	Wed.	Thurs.	Fri.	Sat.

Ear Training _____

Sight Reading _____

Technique _____

_____

_____

_____

Repertoire

_____

_____

_____

_____

_____

_____

_____

_____

_____

_____

_____

_____

_____

_____

_____

Theory _____

Next Lesson _____

Date

	M.M.	Reps.	Sun.	Mon.	Tues.	Wed.	Thurs.	Fri.	Sat.

Ear Training _____

Sight Reading _____

Technique _____

_____

_____

_____

Repertoire

_____

_____

_____

_____

_____

_____

_____

_____

_____

_____

_____

_____

_____

_____

_____

Theory _____

Next Lesson _____

Date

	M.M.	Reps.	Sun.	Mon.	Tues.	Wed.	Thurs.	Fri.	Sat.
Ear Training									
Sight Reading									
Technique									
Repertoire									
Theory									
Next Lesson									

Date

	M.M.	Reps.	Sun.	Mon.	Tues.	Wed.	Thurs.	Fri.	Sat.

Ear Training _____

Sight Reading _____

Technique _____

_____

_____

_____

Repertoire

_____

_____

_____

_____

_____

_____

_____

_____

_____

_____

_____

_____

_____

_____

_____

_____

Theory _____

Next Lesson _____

Date

	M.M.	Reps.	Sun.	Mon.	Tues.	Wed.	Thurs.	Fri.	Sat.

Ear Training _____

Sight Reading _____

Technique _____

_____

_____

_____

Repertoire

_____

_____

_____

_____

_____

_____

_____

_____

_____

_____

_____

_____

_____

_____

Theory _____

Next Lesson _____

© 2015 Barbara M. Siemens PW-5x

Date

	M.M.	Reps.	Sun.	Mon.	Tues.	Wed.	Thurs.	Fri.	Sat.
Ear Training _____									
Sight Reading _____									
Technique _____									
_____									
_____									
_____									

Repertoire

_____

_____

_____

_____

_____

_____

_____

_____

_____

_____

_____

_____

_____

_____

Theory _____

Next Lesson _____

Date

	M.M.	Reps.	Sun.	Mon.	Tues.	Wed.	Thurs.	Fri.	Sat.

Ear Training

Sight Reading

Technique

Repertoire

Theory

Next Lesson

	M.M.	Reps.	Sun.	Mon.	Tues.	Wed.	Thurs.	Fri.	Sat.

Ear Training _____

Sight Reading _____

Technique _____

_____

_____

_____

Repertoire

_____

_____

_____

_____

_____

_____

_____

_____

_____

_____

_____

_____

Theory _____

Next Lesson _____

Date

	M.M.	Reps.	Sun.	Mon.	Tues.	Wed.	Thurs.	Fri.	Sat.

Ear Training _____

Sight Reading _____

Technique _____

_____

_____

_____

Repertoire

_____

_____

_____

_____

_____

_____

_____

_____

_____

_____

Theory _____

Next Lesson _____

Date

		M.M.	Reps.	Sun.	Mon.	Tues.	Wed.	Thurs.	Fri.	Sat.

Ear Training _____

Sight Reading _____

Technique _____

_____

_____

_____

Repertoire

_____

_____

_____

_____

_____

_____

_____

_____

_____

_____

_____

_____

_____

_____

_____

_____

Theory _____

Next Lesson _____

Date

	M.M.	Reps.	Sun.	Mon.	Tues.	Wed.	Thurs.	Fri.	Sat.

Ear Training _____

Sight Reading _____

Technique _____

_____

_____

Repertoire _____

_____

_____

_____

_____

_____

_____

_____

_____

Theory _____

Next Lesson _____

Date

	M.M.	Reps.	Sun.	Mon.	Tues.	Wed.	Thurs.	Fri.	Sat.

Ear Training _____

Sight Reading _____

Technique _____

_____

_____

_____

Repertoire

_____

_____

_____

_____

_____

_____

_____

_____

_____

_____

_____

_____

_____

_____

_____

_____

_____

_____

Theory _____

Next Lesson _____

Date

	M.M.	Reps.	Sun.	Mon.	Tues.	Wed.	Thurs.	Fri.	Sat.
Ear Training									
Sight Reading									
Technique									

Repertoire

Theory _____

Next Lesson _____

Date

	M.M.	Reps.	Sun.	Mon.	Tues.	Wed.	Thurs.	Fri.	Sat.

Ear Training _____

Sight Reading _____

Technique _____

_____

_____

_____

Repertoire

_____

_____

_____

_____

_____

_____

_____

_____

_____

_____

_____

_____

_____

_____

_____

_____

Theory _____

Next Lesson _____

Date

	M.M.	Reps.	Sun.	Mon.	Tues.	Wed.	Thurs.	Fri.	Sat.
Ear Training									
Sight Reading									
Technique									

Repertoire

Theory

Next Lesson

© 2015 Barbara M. Siemens PW-5x

Date

	M.M.	Reps.	Sun.	Mon.	Tues.	Wed.	Thurs.	Fri.	Sat.
Ear Training									
Sight Reading									
Technique									

Repertoire

Theory

Next Lesson

Date

	M.M.	Reps.	Sun.	Mon.	Tues.	Wed.	Thurs.	Fri.	Sat.

Ear Training _____

Sight Reading _____

Technique _____

_____

_____

_____

Repertoire

_____

_____

_____

_____

_____

_____

_____

_____

_____

_____

_____

_____

_____

_____

_____

Theory _____

Next Lesson _____

Date

	M.M.	Reps.	Sun.	Mon.	Tues.	Wed.	Thurs.	Fri.	Sat.

Ear Training _____

Sight Reading _____

Technique _____

_____

_____

_____

Repertoire

_____

_____

_____

_____

_____

_____

_____

_____

_____

_____

_____

_____

_____

_____

Theory _____

Next Lesson _____

Date [   ]

	M.M.	Reps.	Sun.	Mon.	Tues.	Wed.	Thurs.	Fri.	Sat.
Ear Training _____									
Sight Reading _____									
Technique _____									
_____									
_____									
_____									

Repertoire _____									
_____									
_____									

_____									
_____									
_____									

_____									
_____									
_____									

_____									
_____									
_____									

_____									
_____									
_____									

Theory _____

Next Lesson _____

Date

	M.M.	Reps.	Sun.	Mon.	Tues.	Wed.	Thurs.	Fri.	Sat.
Ear Training									
Sight Reading									
Technique									

Repertoire

Theory _____

Next Lesson _____

	M.M.	Reps.	Sun.	Mon.	Tues.	Wed.	Thurs.	Fri.	Sat.

Ear Training _____

Sight Reading _____

Technique _____

_____

_____

_____

Repertoire

_____

_____

_____

_____

_____

_____

_____

_____

_____

_____

_____

_____

_____

_____

_____

_____

Theory _____

Next Lesson _____

© 2015 Barbara M. Siemens PW-5x

Date

	M.M.	Reps.	Sun.	Mon.	Tues.	Wed.	Thurs.	Fri.	Sat.
Ear Training									
Sight Reading									
Technique									

Repertoire

Theory _____

Next Lesson _____

Date

	M.M.	Reps.	Sun.	Mon.	Tues.	Wed.	Thurs.	Fri.	Sat.
Ear Training									
Sight Reading									
Technique									

Repertoire

Theory _____

Next Lesson _____

Date

	M.M.	Reps.	Sun.	Mon.	Tues.	Wed.	Thurs.	Fri.	Sat.

Ear Training _____

Sight Reading _____

Technique _____

_____

_____

_____

Repertoire

_____

_____

_____

_____

_____

_____

_____

_____

_____

_____

_____

_____

_____

_____

_____

_____

_____

Theory _____

Next Lesson _____

Date

	M.M.	Reps.	Sun.	Mon.	Tues.	Wed.	Thurs.	Fri.	Sat.

Ear Training _____

Sight Reading _____

Technique _____

_____

_____

_____

Repertoire

_____

_____

_____

_____

_____

_____

_____

_____

_____

_____

_____

_____

_____

_____

_____

_____

_____

_____

_____

_____

_____

Theory _____

Next Lesson _____

© 2015 Barbara M. Siemens PW-5x

a tempo	return to the previous tempo
accelerando	gradually getting faster
accent >	stress
accidental	flat, sharp, or natural not belonging to the key signature
adagio	at ease, slow - slower than *andante*, faster than *largo*
Alberti Bass	accompaniment pattern common in Classical style works
allegretto	fast but not as fast as *allegro*
allegro	fast, quickly, merrily
andante	at a moderate walking pace
andantino	usually indicates little faster than *andante*
articulation	the style of execution of a note or group of notes, i.e. staccato, legato . . .
cantabile	in a singing style
coda	closing measures or passage
con pedale, ped.	with damper pedal
crescendo, cresc.	gradually louder
da capo, D.C.	repeat from the beginning
dal signo, D.S. ℅	repeat from the sign
damper pedal	right pedal used for sustain or resonance
decrescendo, decresc.	gradually softer
diminuendo, dim.	gradually softer
dolce	sweetly
dominant	fifth note of a scale, V
dynamics	variations in the volume of sound, i.e. loud, soft, etc.
espressivo	expressive
fermata ⌢	pause
fine	the end
forte, f	loud
fortissimo, ff	very loud
grazioso	graceful
imitation	a similar statement of a motive in another voice or hand
larghetto	slow, but not as slowly as *largo*
largo	very slow and solemn
legato	smoothly, connected
lento	slow
leggiero	light
M.M.	Maelzel's Metronome, metronome speed
maestoso	majestic
mano destra, M.D.	right hand
mano sinestra, M.S.	left hand
marcato, marc.	marked or stressed
meno	less
meter	the arrangement of beats into equal measures with regular recurring stresses
mezzo forte, mf	medium loud
mezzo piano, mp	medium soft
moderato	moderate tempo
molto	much, very
motif, **motive**	a short musical idea
ottava 8va	play eight notes higher
8va	play eight notes lower
piano, p	soft
pianissimo, pp	very soft
poco	little
poco a poco	little by little
presto	very fast
prestissimo	as fast as possible
rallentando, rall.	gradually getting slower
repeat sign ‖	indicates a section to be repeated
ritardando, rit.	gradually getting slower
rubato	flexibility in the tempo for expressive purposes
sequence	repeated melodic pattern in the same voice at a higher or lower pitch
sforzando, sf, sfz, fz	a sudden sharp accent
simile	in a similar manner

Music Glossary

slur ⌒	play *legato*, also indicates a phrase or musical idea
solfege	a system using different syllables for each degree of the scale
spiritoso	spirited
staccato	detached
subdominant	fourth note of a scale, IV
subito	suddenly
tempo	speed
tempo primo (tempo I)	return to the original tempo
tenuto ♩	hold note full value; stressed

tie 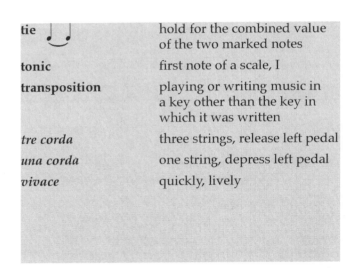	hold for the combined value of the two marked notes
tonic	first note of a scale, I
transposition	playing or writing music in a key other than the key in which it was written
tre corda	three strings, release left pedal
una corda	one string, depress left pedal
vivace	quickly, lively

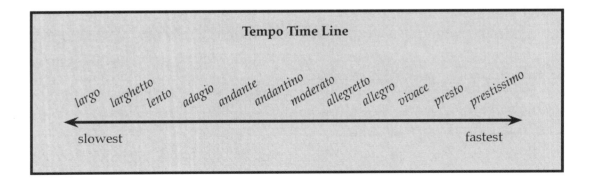

Tempo Time Line

largo larghetto lento adagio andante andantino moderato allegretto allegro vivace presto prestissimo

slowest ← → fastest

Made in the USA
Columbia, SC
31 August 2018